Meanderings In Symbiotic Reality

by

Bob SLaughter

First Edition

Printed by Keystone Book Printing
on recycled materials & manufactured using
electricity partially generated by solar energy

Edited by Zahra Petri
Cover Art by Paul Malachi
Interior Design & Cover Layout by Tracy Peel
Cover Design by Margaret Paine

ISBN: 978-0-578-08281-3

Disclaimer:
The author of this book is not a medical doctor and does not intend for the information to be taken as medical advice. This book is intended for informational purposes only.

Leap of Faith Entities
GreenThePlanet.org

At the core of natural reality
Lies a world of beautiful utility
Sophisticated beyond imagination
Brilliance throughout all creation

Galaxies within a single strand
Infinity at the touch of a hand
Bound in terrain of mind manifest
Yet destined to serenity, beyond our flesh

Traverse egoic constructs of shadowy themes
To gardens of soul, sprouting pure, golden dreams
All waters magically levitating
Life never hesitating

Spontaneous signals throughout the clan
Pure intelligence spells out the plan
Zillions of forms, yet only one
Cosmic design, vast rays of sun

Strife unseen, all is right
Soul purpose, posturing to the light
And all where spirit manifests
Nothing is less and all is blessed

And down in the shadows, the truth hardly lit
Great pain wallows in a gold filled pit
Yet pure math spells the cure
In love, need and greed won't endure

Table of Contents

Introduction

Meanderings In Symbiotic Reality is a collection of writings based in natural intuition, while drawing from scientific understanding. Intuition stems from the Latin word *intueri*, which roughly translated means, to look within or to see within.

Natural suggests nature's influence on our intuitive powers. Science is the process of experimentation, observation, and finally the explanation of the discovered truth or perceived reality, without the influence of preconceived notions.

In the marketing world, under the guise of "science," a "truth" is claimed, then proved through contrived experimentation and/or a biased observation. The truth predetermined for product marketing and/or political purposes, is not at all the TRUTH. In its purest expression, scientific interpretation is still dependent on our limited and sometimes flawed perceptions. Though pure science, when coupled with natural intuition, can help guide us toward TRUTH. As our collective intelligence and spiritual awareness evolves, the effect of deceptive influences dissipates, clarity emerges and we become more creative in addressing our environmental catastrophes and social injustices, and in seeking peaceful solutions to our world's woes.

Our hope is for human consciousness to rise to the occasion, evolve and grow exponentially, as the one great universal, intelligent entity that we are, and come to realize our oneness and our connection to our symbiotic reality, through a melding of heart, mind, soul and intuition, and through communication at even the cellular level. The time is now. Now is of the essence. Our nature is to survive. Our higher nature is to thrive as one human family and beyond as one family of life.

We're All Aliens on This Sphere

Imagine there is a highly evolved society several light years from Earth. Their department of galactic, evolutionary studies has had their eye on planet Earth for some time. They assumed that contact would have occurred by now, but due to Earthlings' inability to transcend violence and greed, that prospect was on hold.

They decided to locate a research specialist on Earth to interact with these humanoids and to gather data to help better understand them. A brilliant woman volunteered, and was accepted for the position. After a short training period and slight physical alterations, she was on her way to Earth. Her credentials and paperwork were spotless due to previously cloaked visits by investigative teams.

She moved into a condo just north of downtown Dallas. Her assimilation went without a hitch. She posed as an Afro/English woman who taught cross cultural and ethnic studies. This well thought out scenario allowed her the room to research for a book, which was the perfect cover for her inter-galactic research. In a short time she learned several languages and was traveling to remote areas of the world. People took to her quite easily. She had an unusual appeal, a quality in her resolve and she spoke forthrightly and honestly.

In her society's quest to achieve ecological balance, they delved deeply into studies of nature's symbiosis. They were compelled to take up intensive studies of mycelial webs and eventually learned to communicate with them. They came to understand that mycelium responds to stimuli with intelligent, honest signals, incapable of deceit, spontaneously acting to resolve impending problems. Their epiphany: brilliance abounds at the cellular level throughout the universe. On her societies' evolutionary path to benevolence, they learned through a variety of non-assuming teachers to transcend their self-destructive ways.

She had to play the Earthling role, remaining incognito, for obvious reasons, the prime directive being at the top of the list. Other than that she was encouraged to be her outgoing self, allowing for a wide degree of creative freedom.

She was taken by the wide spectrum of realities and emotions experienced throughout the world and the stark contrast between very rich and extremely impoverished people. Early on she noticed a strange global syndrome. There was niceness in the demeanor of most wealthy people that she came in contact with. They seemed to be caring, yet they accepted these inequities as inevitable and unavoidable, and they were much too busy with important matters of business to concern themselves beyond fleeting visions for a better world. Someday they would volunteer for a charity, besides they already give so much in tax deductible donations to charities every year.

She found, strangely enough, that working class people possessed similar attitudes, but they were truly consumed by keeping up with an array of payments, seemingly designed to keep them so busy as to never stop and take a breath, ponder and question their reality. When and if one did take the time, their reflection would tend to be tainted with cynicism, a non-effective and self-consuming emotion. People at the bottom of the equation struggled daily to survive another day. They were constantly reminded of their lack of food, water and safety for them and their families.

Though she found an amazing resilience and spirit amongst the very poor, she saw in each class of people a few that stood out as light, beautiful, dedicated, soulful leaders. She knew Earthlings were on a long, arduous, evolutionary journey.

Complications and misunderstandings existed within every mind and every mind set, through every culture and every class. Evolution is a never ending reality, though the important priorities were beginning to reveal themselves. While inequities would surely exist for some time to come, she felt that such planetary suffering had to be addressed immediately.

Having developed close ties with a publisher, she convinced him to publish a series of writings in several languages using a pen name. This series laid out a course of actions that could contribute to the unraveling of Earth's twisted realities and point to solutions, tying corporate success with the lifting up of the world population out of starvation, degradation and homelessness.

It was certain that the innovativeness and resilience of Earthlings, two universal traits of humanoids, could allow for a great metamorphosis to occur. Sorrow and forgiveness seemed to be part of people's daily regime. The Earth seemed like such a strange place, filled with contradictions, yet a vivid reminder of her own people's history. All aspects of human existence were in dire need of alteration. Though at a closer look, there were only a few primary components of this world's dysfunction, spanning all countries, races, religions and classes. Insecurity seemed to be at the root.

She surmised:

- ❖ There is never enough because oneness has yet to be collectively realized. So every individual has to duplicate every need and desire causing shortages of resources and vast pollution. This leads to great alienation, loneliness and mistrust.

- ❖ A lack of trust continually leads to misunderstandings, and perpetual conspiracy theories of worst possible intentions.

- ❖ Greed takes on a life of its own; a never ending quest for material wealth that can never satisfy one's inner yearnings.

- ❖ Fear of losing everything and of having nothing contributes to divisiveness, the "me or him" syndrome, curbing the realization of our oneness. All isms are allowed to fester into hatred without this shared realization: religion-ism, racism, classism, ageism, sexism.

So many complicated issues, yet all stemming from this simple seed of insecurity, a lacking amongst great abundance and infinite possibilities.

She knows that truth is the fertilizer of change, but without a sense of compassion for all, it will never heal the deep wounds caused by misunderstanding, hatred and greed.

She sits down and begins to write:
"Taking a chance to speak one's truth risks ridicule and even persecution. Yet communication and the sharing of perspectives will help to facilitate understanding and collective vision. All is of the cosmos. Once there was no Earth. We are all aliens on this sphere, yet we all are sentient beings, connected through consciousness..."

Waking Up

Imagine this scenario: There is a woman, a kind-hearted individual, who after reading a book about Gandhi, decided to prepare some rather grandiose resolutions for the New Year. Gandhi's quote, "you must be the change you wish to see in the world", resonated strongly with her and took up permanent residence in her consciousness.

As winter solstice and New Year's celebrations ensued, she turned her focus to her friends and family. It was a particularly festive year's end. She arose on January 2nd with a sense of empowerment and directive. Though recently she had been feeling some sort of soul movement was under way, something within her had shifted. She woke to a resounding realization of oneness. She pulled out her list of resolutions and smiled as she reviewed her goals:

- ❖ Work for world peace
- ❖ End starvation and afford shelter for all
- ❖ Stop poisoning the earth
- ❖ Care for all children
- ❖ Slow the frantic pace of animal and plant extinction

She thought, "Wow, that's ambitious!" Then she remembered what a friend had once told her, "there are no delusions of grandeur. They are dreams of empowerment, metaphorical seeds. Not all are planted, fewer sprout, even fewer grow."

With that recollection, she spun into action. With two phone calls she was sipping tea and sharing her experience with a couple of friends. They were fascinated with her resolve. To her surprise, they didn't even blink an eye. They decided to meet once a week for breakfast at a local cafe.

As friends became aware of their activities, their group grew larger. The founders had developed several precepts that they insisted be adhered to. They knew they did not want to control the group, only maintain the initial integrity.

The resolutions became the group's goals. The precepts included adherence to:

- ❖ Honesty and open mindedness while attempting to unravel complicated issues
- ❖ Soul purpose as the basis for decisions
- ❖ A respectful, yet secular approach, with an emphasis on our commonalities
- ❖ Each equation would include the standard consideration, "for the greater good of all"

The founder's niece caught wind and spun a circle of young folks at a coffee house near campus. Social status, income brackets and ethnicity mattered not. Each group's talent pool was broad and rich. The younger group adopted and customized similar precepts and began a collective truth quest and a plan of action of their own. Both groups developed their own websites and blogs, which connected to a larger collective forum that was spreading as natural as signals running through a mycelial web.

Each group's curiosity of the other remained heightened and they were able to learn and draw from perspectives across social, political, economic and racial lines.

So many environmental, political and social justice groups were springing up everywhere, so they decided to start with their broad worldly goals and work their way inward towards the details of action. This created a link between many specific groups as resources for education and activism in the realms of politics, environment, health and local agriculture, organic buying clubs, self-help programs, honest relief organizations, etc.

This is one of several basic organic scenarios that has shown to be a natural template for those wishing to start their own groups. Will, endurance, mutual respect and a commitment to goals and precepts, are keys to a group's success.

As so many scenarios continue to unfold, the big question is— who will achieve critical mass first, the forces of darkness or evolving love consciousness?

A Day in the Life

Imagine you wake up one day and no longer view the world through a filter. You see everything as it really is. You draw a hot bath; you see the hot water heater pulling electricity down the wires from the coal plant. You watch thoughts arise that you discard as unconscious, programmed streams, realizing that you do not own them. You prepare breakfast from food that has been picked by immigrant farm workers and journeyed long distances to rest in your fridge, then make its way through your intestinal tract, to a treatment plant where the residue finally rests upon the banks of your local river.

Is this new awareness a gift or a curse? That will depend on what you do with it.

You turn on the TV to catch the morning news. You realize the corporate sponsors have an agenda and have infected the content of the broadcast. After brushing your teeth with a sugary paste on petroleum based bristles, you grab a plastic bottle of water and head out the door. You turn the key of your car, igniting gas that has been refined from a mixture of worldly oil, a karmic blend, whose origins are impossible to know. Cruising past signs of programming, you are no longer enticed to yield to urges of addictive behavior patterns. You pass by all temptations.

You pull into the parking garage. Where on earth did they get all of this concrete? You ascend to your cubicle. You work and you communicate on desktop and handheld devices until lunch.

Knowing the answers, you still frame them in the form of questions. How can they make so much stuff in China? Why is it cheaper by the time they have made it and shipped it all the way over here?

Lunch brings to mind images of a farmer's broken dreams, sued out of business by Monsanto's lawyers for infringement of GMO seed patents. You wonder, when justice prevails, what will happen to all of Monsanto's employees. You realize when that time comes to pass we will no longer be in the days of Enron, and retraining programs and reassignments will become available for all.

A cohort snaps his fingers and you return to your lunch and their conversation. Err on the side of caution or wild abandon? There is no right answer, but for now, you talk football.

Lunch is over, stocks are bought and sold, deals are made, decisions infect reality.

You are finally home. Peace of mind is what you want for dinner. You walk, stretch, sit, reflect, contemplate, meditate. You see that peace is an inward journey and that its outward manifestation may come in time.

You sleep like a baby and rise to a brand new day, knowing you will begin to share with others.

A Note from the Author

Now a truth quest is in order. Not my truth or your truth, but universal TRUTH. There is a conscious revolution under way and I am merely throwing my seven sense in the ring as well. I wish to be open and kind hearted in our quest, yet remain adhered to honesty. If you feel insulted by the words that follow, I am truly sorry. That is not my intention. I have attempted to soften my language the best I know how. We are in a time of great change, teetering between peril and exaltation. We need to take a look at the brutal truth to end brutality.

The Truth Prescription

All truth passes through three stages.
First, it is ridiculed.
Second, it is violently opposed
Third, it is accepted as being self-evident.
Arthur Schopenhauer

If you have been sleeping and are beginning to wake up to reality, your experience might be somewhat similar to that of the person in "A Day in the Life."

To sleep through life might seem like a good way to avoid such a harsh reality, for facing the truth is like accepting the pain. Believing the lies is like taking drugs to numb the pain.

The journey to a beautiful reality travels directly through the center of the pain. We can allow ourselves to feel the pain and know the truth.

The truth prescription begins with a media fast. Take a break from the news, the TV shows, the advertising… the world can wait. Begin a truth quest. Allow questions to arise. **What is true? Can truth be known? Are there people who do not want you to understand the truth?** You may discover that you have emotional attachments to non-truths, to fabrications propagated by corporate government interests or even by anti-corporate government interests. Broaden the quest to all matters of the spirit. Question our perceived reality. **Is it wrong for people to suffer in the midst of such prosperity? Can we afford basic rights and comforts to all of the world citizens? Is this our duty? Can kindness and love conquer hatred and greed?** Many questions may surface during media fasts and truth quests.

It is likely not possible to return to corporate sponsored, mass media news without being taken in and tricked into aligning with or against their agenda once again. They can be very clever in their performance.

There are alternatives to mainstream news. Find your true, objective self, and you can find your source for non-biased information.

As you return to the news of harsh realities of our world, you may want to ease into it. After hearing a report on a devastating situation like in Haiti, Gaza or Afghanistan, on a particular injustice and/or an environmental catastrophe, allow some time to process the information. Go for a jog or a long walk, do some yoga, meditate, contemplate. Consider solutions. Discuss issues with friends. Perhaps you can find common ground. If you feel you are becoming cynical, you may be taking in news from a biased source or you may be overwhelmed by too much intense information.

We all have our own tolerance level, though we can train our psyche to absorb more of our world's reality. The key to balance is involvement in solutions, sharing ideas, finding creative forms of expression, while finding and maintaining peace with oneself.

One might think truth is rather subjective. However, as our scientific understanding evolves and our intuitive powers develop through meditating and spending time in nature, by being propaganda free, and just being willing to be honest with ourselves, we can become capable of screening information down to purer forms of truth. And of course this ride is a collective experience. We are all in this together.

In determining the purity of truth, one might ask, "does the radio or TV station, newspaper, blog, journalist or writer receive payments from a corporate entity, from anyone with invested interest in the subject matter?" If we pull our ego and our own personal interest out of the equation, we can use our better judgment to determine someone's commitment to truth. To see truth, we must be honest with ourselves. Truth is pure and real. It has no hidden agenda. It is merely **what is**.

Those in charge of the corporate world, have much interest at stake in their investments and endeavors. They can't be trusted to tell the truth. Their power base ranges from ownership of TV and radio networks and stations, to newspapers, to huge corporate investments in oil, coal, nuclear, pharmaceuticals, agriculture, weaponry, etc., to lobbying activities, to holding political office. Some truth seeps through sometimes, but only a small percent is allowed through or slips under their radar. From its inception, television has served the corporate government elite well. What a propaganda tool, and now the screens are bigger and better than ever.

TV, radio and computers are great tools for inspiration, for revealing our commonalities, for learning about the many cultures of our world, as well as our beautiful and complex universe, and for shedding light on the injustices and environmental challenges that we face. Electronic media is necessary to our survival; however, watching fictitious images of needless violence and despair, and being continually hit on to buy this gizmo and that piece of junk, can contribute to a state of confusion and dis-ease.

Instead of buying their stuff to fuel our addictive behavior, we can walk away and put our trust in nature and the natural processes, and in our natural intuitive abilities. Cleanse the junk from our minds, the residual visuals. Enjoy fasting from your TV. To do so can be very empowering. The freed mind may never again return to corporate media sources.

There are news sources that practice honest journalism. There is a revolution in journalism these days. It is important to know what our governments, corporate heads, banksters and power brokers are up to in the world in order to develop our collective strategies. To allow the militarization of the world in our name is not acceptable. In the presence of truth, our collective spirit can flourish. We can form partnerships across borders. We can return the human operations of the world to the people at the grassroots level. We can unite for fairness, justice and equality.

We can seek truth without getting lost in the darkness, cynicism, racism, this ism and that ism. Light reflects light. One can study and delve into the darkness, but live in the light. If there is more peace in our hearts, there is more peace in the world.

Self empowerment, thus collective empowerment evolves from a quest for truth. Sheltering one's self from harsh truths and realities might seem to allow protection from mental, emotional and physical stress and dis-ease; however, to strengthen one's ability to face such truths is part of the regimen that can lead to a holistic health and balance.

Add in a bit of truth serum to a daily diet of clean living, mineral rich organic foods and herbs, pure water and air, exercise, meditation, purposeful endeavors and service to life, and the truth surely won't over power these good, healthy influences to the body, heart, mind, emotions, soul and spirit. Soul capacity and the flow of spirit will surely grow, as will resolve.

Self Empowerment/ Collective Empowerment

Strength does not come from physical capacity.
It comes from an indomitable will.
Mahatma Gandhi

To realize that we have been taken advantage of, lied to, that opinions have been formulated from false information, certainly can be disheartening, but can also be a necessary step up to self-empowerment, thus a step towards collective empowerment.

We are all in this together, and I mean everyone. Each individual shifting into new paradigms of understanding and compassion, adds to the likelihood, that with the quantum shift occurring in this time, we will manifest a new earth, where heart and soul vibrations become the dominant influence.

Will we come to terms with the fact that the corporate governments of imperialism propagate misinformation to further their agenda? And a dark agenda it is. The spin of its goodness is forever embellished, confusing its want to believers, perhaps many of whom are otherwise descent people who tend to believe what they are told through their media sources.

"Question authority" is always a good motto to keep in mind. A true understanding of our story, not white washed versions of his-story, will allow us to disbelieve information from corporate government, mass media sources. Though there is no need to be disenchanted, for beauty and honesty abounds in our human race, and the truth can be empowering.

Not What It Seems?

Factions of the fundamentalist Christian Right, under the guise of Christianity and /or political revolution, such as the billionaire Koch brothers' Tea Party, and the minutemen mentality, are attracting people who have been disenfranchised from traditional American reality.

A kind of fascism is offered as a sort of comfort in place of a stable family life. As people lose their jobs, their health care, their homes, some become vulnerable to manipulation and propaganda. The drug of racist hatred may seem to ease the pain by blaming the immigrant workers or the Chinese slave labor force, yet such scapegoating plays into the hands of the international bankers, the corporate heads and their politicos.

It's necessary to know who the actual perpetrators of economic disparity are, while learning to avoid the blame and the self-victimization.

Everyone has the potential for change, yet some may never change. Change is always a personal journey and positive change tends to occur through loving kindness. Organic change begins in our own community, in the workplace, the coffee houses, bars, churches, social events, etc. Be bold. Be brave. Say what you feel. Love is powerful. People will tend to agree with honest, well thought out, kindhearted logic more than reactionary, desperate and angry ideas.

How can the hard working Latino community from south of the border be responsible for so much job loss when the same corporations, the same people who out sourced so many jobs from the US are responsible for gutting the economies of the countries that they immigrated from?

You can't logically argue with points like that. Answers can be found in bridge building, making connections, grassroots organizing and grassroots economic development. We can take over the works of the world. When people are taken care of and are allowed to take care of themselves, they no longer have a use for hatred.

The tactic for dealing with those powerful hate mongers who don't seem to have the capacity to change their ways, is to go about the business of taking back our power, our economies, our governments and our churches. We can hold out hope for everyone without holding our breath.

The age of the flower child has passed, yet that love power remains the foundation of this: the age of truth and soul consciousness. It's the fire feeding this revolution of the heart.

Politics as Unusual

The will of the people is the only legitimate foundation of any government, and to protect its free expression should be our first object.

Thomas Jefferson

Politics tends to serve the ruling class. In our culture that class is the upper echelon of the corporate power structure. The terms left wing and right wing suggest wings of a single bird. That bird is the corporate government elite. The wings serve to divide the people into constantly debating factions, when in reality we all have so much in common; our basic survival needs, our desire for comfort, security, health, longevity, peace and a sense of community.

Our one common enemy, greed, allows the corporate world to keep us struggling to stay above water. While our two major parties espouse two different philosophies, they both support and are supported by the most powerful corporations in the world. There is little wonder why positive change, especially from the federal level, is so elusive.

If left unchecked for too long, an educated and powerful middle class would spell the end of the ruling class as we know it. Very few times in the history of the United States, did power begin shifting to the middle class. Corporate government leaders were ousted, wars were ended, and our country's wealth began to benefit the masses.

As this last great American Revolution came to a close, the conservative think-tankers went to work, and successfully repaired their wounds and retook much of their lost ground. Unfortunately, those who control TV, radio and the printed word have controlled the masses, though the Internet has become our greatest weapon since LSD during the hippy revolution.

Lies, misconceptions and fortunately truth, travel at the speed of electrons. That is good news because when given a chance, truth and reason tend to win over lies and deception.

Truth is a component of love, for true love wants what is right, real, fair and just. Being that we are one conscious entity, it is our higher nature to desire the best for us all. Our mindsets need to be shaken up. Our cages need an intense rattling. We are stuck as actors in his-story, pawns in a game of chess. To understand how we have been played the fool, is to begin to step beyond denial, to pass through anger and resentment, to acceptance of reality and on to a revolution of the heart; a journey into truth and change for the collective betterment.

Disgruntled Ghosts

In the darkness of humanity, billions of lives have been shortened or taken through disregard or outright murder and pillage; all that energy prematurely sent back to the ethers. The karmic debt is huge. It will be paid. As this debt is prolonged, we storm to the brink, where we could be swallowed by Mother Earth as were prehistoric dinosaurs.

The Beast

The beast lurks within the darkness, within our shadow. It is greed and hatred. It is fear, jealousy, envy, lust, denial, etc. The unconscious and unsuspecting are easily tricked and drawn into its web, for to hate hatred is to summon the beast. As much as we would rather not admit, we all contribute to the manifestations of darkness, with our unconscious emotions.

We all have been overshadowed by our collective, unconscious, dark side. People within the uncaring corporate/elitist/government power structure, as well as many who rail against this massive structure, those in hate groups and "terrorist" organizations, soldiers, officers and mercenaries are not the beast, per se, but have become servants to the expressions of darkness, misguided from their soul purpose, overwhelmed by their shadow.

Thus, an attempt to slay the beast as an external force actually feeds that energy. Slaying the beast suggests an inward journey, discovering the demons within our own psyche, within our own egoic reality, and rather than eliminating and banishing the beast from our depths, like cleansing toxins from our body, perhaps the answer is to merely lift our consciousness beyond the darkness. We don't own this invisible force. We unconsciously allow it to inhabit our psyche. To shed light on our shadow, is to become conscious of its aspects.

Rather than being doomed to follow or be followed by our metaphorical shadow, it might be that we are just stuck in a lower nature duality. As prisoners of mental concepts, it is easy to blame the obvious culprits, the rich and powerful, for example. But within that assignment of blame lies a flawed strategy.

It is being suggested that we have the potential to collectively transcend this duality through evolving soul consciousness. If good must be bound with evil to exist, perhaps such concepts no longer serve us. Higher consciousness rises above duality. Where there is no egoic judgment, duality falls away leaving matters of the heart and soul. No longer needing to label, rate and value reality, we are free to discover our collective strategies for peace building and dismantling the war profiteering machine.

As we search deep within ourselves, and honestly peel away the layers of dark, subconscious suppressions, we come in contact with old deposits of emotional residue from regrettable activities of our past, of situations we were unable to consciously process at the time. As we take a stark look at our emotional past, we begin to develop a better understanding of who we really are. To realize our whole self is to understand our true potential, an act of self empowerment.

Through this process we can gain empathy for our adversaries, the perpetrators of the physical acts of darkness. The ones most responsible for the pain and suffering on our planet are those trapped at the deepest levels of their shadow. Those most unconscious of their emotional history, their shadow, their karma, are together carrying out organized acts of inexplicable horror. We must understand the nature of their pain to know how to defuse their influence and how to circumvent their power.

His-story or Our-story

If they can get you asking the wrong questions,
they don't have to worry about the answers.
Thomas Pynchon

From time immemorial, human conquest has wreaked havoc upon nomads and villagers. To this day such an imperialistic mentality threatens indigenous people and old, well rooted cultures worldwide. There is no doubt that tools of propaganda have always been employed to maintain the status quo.

As each act of state sponsored terror is committed, his-story begins to revise and white wash the account, forever spinning the non-reality. No matter how absurd the stories would become, the propaganda would normally keep the majority complicit with the government-sponsored horrors of the day. There have been rebellions and revolutions from time to time, but the powers to be have usually managed to ultimately circumvent them.

Our stories of medical malpractice, home foreclosures, relief donations squandered and stolen and governmental and institutional indifference are the fertilizer for grassroots change, allowing for collective recognition of what is wrong.

Our stories of community windmills, cooperative reconstruction, organic home gardens watered by solar powered rainwater catchment systems, health recaptured through the use of organic and wild foods, super foods and super herbs, fasting, body/mind therapies, acupuncture, earthing, and so many non-evasive, natural healing practices, help erode fallacies of propaganda, leading the way to a holistic reality.

A Response to Racism

There was a single ancestral group of organisms, and some split off to become fungi and some split off to become animals. The latter have become us.
Microbiologist Mitchell Sogin

Who was here first? What is the life lineage? Who has the right to claim this earth, to claim this land we call the United States?

Fungi predated animal life. It was presumably one of the main survivors of an asteroid collision and the resulting darkness that ensued some 250 million years ago and again some 65 million years ago. Following this last major asteroid collision, plant and animal life reemerged, evolved and thrived during these many millions of years of pre-humanoid reality.

As humanoid life evolved, nomadic humans made their way to the farthest reaches of the world. They began to inhabit the "Americas" some thirty-five thousand years ago, a relatively short period in geological time. The ensuing indigenous relationship between human, plant, animal and fungal life forms was for the most part, symbiotic and mutually beneficial. So in the western hemisphere "Native Americans" became the rightful human, benevolent caretakers and coordinators of the wilderness gardens of life.

With the arrival of "western man" and their mentality of brutal imperialism, over five hundred years ago, a mere blink in geologic time, the balance of life immediately began to shift. As this western mentality moved across the Americas, vast disruptions to the ecological balance occurred at an ever-increasing rate, which continues to this day.

The human ego tends to lay claim, define his domain, trap his prey, fence in his ill-gotten land, and consume all resources in sight for his supposed enrichment. And in short time, believes he is the sole and rightful owner of his property, certainly an alien concept to his indigenous predecessors.

Racism is an extension of such egoic concepts and practices. It is, and always was, obsolete. To heal racism would be to heal the earth, for we cannot cause harm to anyone or any other life form without causing harm to ourselves: body and/or psyche.

The great environmental imbalance is a reflection of the human imbalance between mind/ego and truth/reality. These belief systems, based in non-reality, attempt to divide our oneness, which cannot be done. Therefore it falls under the definition of insanity. There is no justification for white supremacy and white privilege, or for the supremacy and privilege of any other color, class or religious group, for that matter.

Are We a Program?

Complicity with corporate government and media-sponsored terror has a huge adverse effect on our psychic health and in turn our holistic wellness. If we step outside of who we think we are, we can find out how we actually feel about ourselves and the world around us.

Our highly subsidized, corporate industries manifest their agenda by controlling mass media and the electoral process, programming enough of the population to avoid revolution and their expulsion. Strike up a spirited debate about the corporate power structure and war profiteering, and you will see a lot of programmed, knee jerk reactions to realistic, logical, compassionate views.

If a fast food restaurant is built and begins serving a toxic, genetically modified, charred substance for their main ingredient, with radiated potatoes on the side, then people begin to flock in and chow down. Marketing has refined its skills to a tee. Should you trust their word? Should you trust any mass marketed product or concept? Only if in money, you trust the most.

Early in our nation's story, corporations were allowed to form only to accomplish a specific goal, to build a bridge or a canal or some other activity that at least seemingly benefitted the public. When the task was complete, the corporation was required to dismantle. Thomas Jefferson and his cohorts knew all too well the dangers of allowing corporations to take on a life of their own.

Now corporate power is entwined with our government and its policies. Corporations are not going away, so it's best we learn to program corporations to exist for people instead of the other way around.

Buttons

Ego buttons are subconscious trigger points. When pushed by particular stimuli, they cause emotional reactions which stem from deep rooted feelings that can go back to early childhood, and include all influences to present day. The psychology of marketing targets these points to sell ideas, convince people that they need a particular product or that they should adopt a particular belief, whether it be political, philosophical or religious. The science of marketing has become so highly refined that we don't realize how programmed we truly are to have a particular belief or reaction.

Consider words like communism, socialism, capitalism, racism, ageism, sexism, Christian, Muslim, Hindu, Buddhist, vegetarian, GMO, peace, war, bankers, hippy, redneck, yuppie, liberal, conservative, environmentalist, Bush, Obama, Ralph Nader, Glenn Beck, Halliburton, Enron, cancer, gay sex, tea party, Al-Qaeda, illegal alien, and the death penalty. Dig deep and write down whatever words or phrases spark an emotional response, then delve, as deep as you can, into your subconscious to understand its source. Can you trace this surfaced emotional residue back to a past experience, or series of experiences, that caused emotions to lodge and stagnate within the body or psyche? If we are honest with ourselves and remain conscious of our feelings, we can conduct an ongoing examination and stay in touch with the under lying sources of our feelings. The more we bring our subconscious feelings to the surface, the less we are vulnerable to outside interference, and the more likely our buttons will fade away.

Optimism or Cynicism

If you realized how powerful your thoughts are,
you would never think a negative thought.
Peace Pilgrim

Take your pick, it's a state of mind: *half empty* or *half full.* I choose optimism. I say we will enter into a new age, a new paradigm, where love and kindness rule. As you line up to place your bets, what outcome do you wish for? What do you stand for, life or death, lightness or darkness? Choose your favorite. Pick your horse and place your bet, and you might as well believe you are going to win. That is favoring optimism.

You can be a realist, face the beast, know the truth, and still believe in a positive outcome. Such an attitude can't hurt. Hope is our only real hope. If we are defeatist, then we are defeated.

If you are cynical and feel that things can't change for the better, or if you just don't give a damn, except perhaps for your own immediate family and friends, then you are part of the problem. Complacency is complicity. For positive global change to occur, we must believe it can, and we must go about the business of correcting the problems that stem from greed, indifference and lust for power, as well as addressing the roots of these insecurities.

Forgiveness

To forgive is to set a prisoner free and
discover that the prisoner was you.
Lewis B. Smedes

Faulting and blaming others, be they people, political parties, countries, races or classes, is a habitual activity, emotionally charged and often ill conceived. It has been determined that the mind has as many as 80,000 thoughts a day. Unless we consciously quiet the mind, we must endure a constant chatter throughout each day. Within that chatter resides all of the dysfunction, the subconscious blame that plays out in our world theater. The collective ego has never reached such proportions.

If you feel that someone has done you wrong, that someone may feel the same about you. It's the ego that wants to hold onto grievances and run them around in your head continually, making sure that you know that you were right and they were wrong. You can't be happy with such nonsense playing out in your mind.

You may find that if you forgive yourself, it is easier to forgive someone else. It's a form of love. To forgive requires a movement to the higher self. It comes from the heart and soul, from a desire for a better, more humane world.

The time has come when we can move out of personal and collective denial. The movement has been occurring and is escalating. It is part of the greater paradigm shift. Peace requires forgiveness. It would serve those of us in the peace and justice movement well, to nurture peace and forgiveness within our hearts. Demonizing our adversaries is not appropriate or productive. We need to know truth and still feel love for all. One without the other is inadequate.

To harbor ill feelings towards someone is to disallow one's own peace of mind and solitude. Forgiveness serves the forgiver and the forgiven. Most of us have held on to petty grievances for far too long, sometimes to the point of forgetting the initial dispute. However, there are great role models who have endured acts of brutality towards themselves, and/or their family and friends, and still have found it within their hearts to forgive. We can all cultivate such power of love to overcome the great barriers to peace and justice in our times.

Judgment Calls

As we evolve spiritually, we can see that passing judgment on individuals accomplishes nothing. In order to improve our condition and move to a sustainable and loving reality, it is helpful to distinguish between passing judgment on people and passing judgment on people's actions, decadent and unsustainable lifestyles, obsolete endeavors, such as war, and acquisition and development of non-renewable resources.

To know what is wrong is a step towards determining what is right. We can no longer tolerate destructive practices for the sake of jobs. That is an old school, corporate hierarchy mentality. We are more creative than that. It is easy to blame politicians and executives for our problems. It is more practical to be aware of the mistakes and move on to positive solutions. It seems likely that we will continue to implement many of these solutions on our own at the grassroots level, as we work to reign in our corporate government.

Wealth

Wealth is the ability to fully experience life.
Henry David Thoreau

Wealth encompasses it all, from the obvious accumulations in the material realm to more ethereal & spiritual accomplishments, both personal and collective. If the personal accumulation of stuff becomes a selfish endeavor, beyond the seeking of basic comforts, and neglectful of the needs of others (both human and non-human), if there is a desire to acquire in order to achieve happiness, then happiness remains elusive and our collective wealth is diminished.

Therefore, personal wealth cannot be separated from collective betterment, a physical and conscious evolution of our world community. By meeting our material needs and desires and in turn meeting the demands to bring some equity to human kind and to balance our ecology, new ways are emerging in the design and development of more naturalized living structures, renewable energy generation, and blending gardens of delight and nutrition with natural wilderness. Symbiotic reality can flow throughout neighborhoods, communities and rural areas on private and public lands.

Consider wealth to be connected, symbiotic, evolutionary, expansive systems inherent in natural design, inherent in nature. We as humans could learn much from a fruit tree. From its inception, a fruit tree becomes a very productive entity. It has many positive effects such as being a protective canopy for other plants and animals by providing shade, easing heavy rainfall and hail, nurturing the soil, plants, and animals with its composting leaves and branches, fallen buds and fruits, and sharing its pollen with bees and butterflies as they pollinate other tree's blossoms.

All emissions from its production are useful sources of nutrients, or in some way nurturing to other life forms. There is no toxic pollution, unless introduced by humans, such as pesticides or chemical fertilizers. This is a highly wealthy, symbiotic situation that we can learn to emulate. It offers insight into the realm of infinite possibilities, of a practically infinitely unfolding abundance on Earth, pointing the way to a world without war and poverty, eliminating any excuses for allowing suffering on our planet.

A wealth of shared spirit manifests on the physical plane. A highly abundant, nurtured Earth spirit shows itself in the form of beautiful, sustainable, healthy dwellings, scattered throughout the natural landscape of fields and woods, parks and gardens, fruit trees and nut trees, wild edibles everywhere, bees, butterflies and birds, frogs, turtles and lizards, and so on. Potentially all human and non-human needs could be met in this symbiotic reality.

Wealth encompasses intuitive wisdom, understanding that we *are* nature, inside and out. It doesn't start here and stop there, nor do we.

A wealth of excitement comes alive with each rising soul awakened by the ever-rising sun, each day encouraged by continual growing support systems multiplying in our consciousness, manifesting in our reality.

In nature there is no unemployment and no unnecessary hunger. Relief from natural disasters would be immediately summoned and suffering minimized through human kindness. That is wealth.

Let the Money Flow and Your Wealth Will Grow

As the temporary tax cuts for the rich become more permanent, social safety nets continue to fray and the potential for economic stimulus from government declines. The rich have tended to spend a much smaller percentage of their money on goods and services and big money has not been investing in smart sustainable startups that train people to earn living wages.

Our economy is stagnant. "Reagan's trickle down" barely drops pittances into a growing number of pockets. A tiny segment of our population has succeeded in damming up a large percentage of the money, a short-term financial success for them, as they fall into spiritual dysfunction and karmic peril.

The amount of time spent pursuing money distracts us from other important activities such as lending a hand to less fortunate people, gardening, communing with nature and meditating. It can be such a joy sharing your homegrown produce, flowers, music and art with people.

Once we understand the breadth of wealth, it becomes easier to allow our monetary wealth to flow out into the community, for it ripples back in the form of love and gratitude, not to mention the potential financial returns. In every aspect of life there are innumerable possibilities waiting to be brought into reality.

The smart money seeks to fertilize progressive ideas, aiding in their inception, and helping them come to fruition, to a life of their own. What a blessing it is for someone to be financially wealthy and to have the wealth of heart, mind and spirit. Just let the fun continue. Every morning brings delightful possibilities.

Micro lending has emerged as a very successful economic strategy for struggling people in developing countries. These low interest, unsecured loans have a payback rate of approximately 98%.

Now that interest rates on investments have tanked, perhaps 3% payback will emerge as the new standard, and much great work could come from flowing money at that rate. It diminishes the concept of usage and could potentially level the playing field. Ultimately it might not even be a game that we play, but rather a compassionate reality that we create. We can grow trees and forests where they are no longer. We can aid in the return of creeks and rivers, and the fauna and flora that would inevitably return to live in such natural habitats. We can offer hope to people with none. There is no greater purpose than nurturing hope, growing trees, cleansing the air and water, aiding in the recovery of natural environments and transferring the human works of the world back to the hands of the people, thus shifting from routines of darkness to joyous pursuits of enlightened endeavors.

Lucrative Design

We can't merely go about our business, and leave the corporate heads and international banksters to their own devices. Plans must be offered that point to lucrative designs, mutually beneficial relationships with investors, developers and workers. Through propagating and growing renewable wealth, resources and resourcefulness in the world, we can make enough riches to go around.

There is great wealth in natural balance. The key is to live with wealth, not to personalize it or take it away. Ultimately the need for money could disappear. One of the great benefits for the rich is uplifted spirit, an increase in the wealth of spirit, love and kindness and good karma.

In a renewable green economy wealth is regenerated. We can let go of the concept of limited resources. There can be plenty to go around.

There becomes a point where less is more. It takes a lot to house loneliness and selfishness. Continual longings are never appeased. The purer heart, mind and body, places less demands on the material world, and tends to offer more in return.

We Are What We Are

We are what we eat. We are what we think. We are what we dream. Every nutrient, toxin, thought, karmic event, sensual stimulus, decision, influence, whether it be physical, ethereal, large or small, all add up to who we are. Everything matters, material and virtual. We are evolving cosmic debris.

Body Heart Mind Soul Spirit

All is one. Body, Heart, Mind, Soul and Spirit are concepts, mere words, used in an attempt to understand parts of the whole. It is not clear where one ends and another begins, because they are all connected, as all human vessels are interconnected as one societal entity. We all share Body, Heart, Mind, Soul and Spirit with each other.

Even the body is not a solid, as we once thought. It is a small ocean, housing vast space, vibrating at many frequencies and containing pathways of electrons. The body is an extension of the earth, pulsating to the heavens.

The body is the physical vessel for the heart, and the host of the mind and soul. The mind and soul are localized in and around the body, yet are not limited by physical boundaries or distance. The body is an expression and a celebration of the physical universe. We are celestial creatures receiving sustenance from celestial bodies, the Earth and beyond.

Where does the physical end and the meta-physical or ethereal begin? Does quantum entanglement suggest interconnectedness through space and time? We are all one, what does that really mean? Does it mean physically or metaphorically? Would it change our feelings towards one another to find that we are physically interconnected? Or is the physical of the least importance? Certainly we are interconnected through consciousness, through heart vibrations and through mental and emotional vibrations.

The intelligence of the body at the cellular level spontaneously signals and activates necessary functions to maintain a resilient balance, to thrive and to survive foreign viral and bacterial invasions. It stands to reason that the rest of our being has similar collective intelligence and capability.

So our connectedness to the Earth body suggests that the entire Earth system is one life or one entity, one web of life, one symbiotic reality. As our civilization grasps such concepts, we begin to find it impossible to destroy our Earth-Self and will stop at nothing to alter our destructive activities and heal and repair our body.

The heart is of course of the body, yet beats to a rhythm that is beyond the body, that of the Earth, and no doubt of a universal pulse, of cosmic energy. A healthy heart is in sync with the rhythm of the Earth and resonates with vibrations of love and kindness.

It would seem that our collective rhythm is jumbled, out of rhythm, out of sync, hence the confusion on our planet. There is collective heart dis-ease. Some of the neediest of hearts dwell in the richest of bodies. We are experiencing a dysfunctional collective heart, disconnected from natural reality, truth-realty and from our soul purpose, that of creative expression of love and kindness, which is integral in the healing of the Earth-Body and in restoring and maintaining balance.

The mind is the seer of visions, organizer of intelligence, decider of plans and tactics. The healthy, pure state of mind is a meditative awareness utilizing mental capacities for the furtherance of life and universal consciousness. The silent, seeing mind can facilitate the flowing of spirit through soul and intellectually understand our oneness, the inter-connected, collective Body, Heart, Mind, Soul and Spirit.

Spending time in nature or in natural settings allows the mind to experience stillness, tranquility, calmness, and peace. Spirit can grow and prosper in such an environment. Our purpose can unfold and service can be planned and realized.

The soul is stationed in and around one's body, but certainly not limited to it. It is a receiver and an amplifier of spirit. It resonates with spirit and with cosmic consciousness. It is of the local, as well as of the non-local I. Similar to mind, and you could say connected with mind, soul thought is based in heart, not head. Like merging water droplets, soul, as is spirit, is ethereal fluidity.

As we learn to cleanse the toxins from our body, our desire grows to cleanse the Earth Mother of the toxins that we have stirred up in the environment. Our connection to the Mother, our realization of oneness, a vast, infinite universal and expanding reality, grows through infinite imagination and possibilities. We are gardeners of heart, miners of love and sculptors of kindness and loving feelings. Such activity nurtures our body, heart, mind and soul as much as the finest organic living food cuisine. They go hand in hand. Clean, living foods resonate at a high level with an evolving human. The less energy that is required to digest food, the more energy there is available for higher purposes, and there are higher purposes for us all. Feed the body mostly pure, living, organic and wild foods, clean air and pure water. Feed the heart and soul pure vibrations of love and caring for our fellow humans, as well as all other life forms.

As we cleanse and nurture the body, feel the heart and open all of the chakras to the great energy flow, while quieting the mind through meditation, and understanding it as a tool of consciousness in partnership with the body, heart and soul, an integrated reality opens up within our individual selves and our collective self.

Our health and survival is dependent on the health of the greater Earth-Body, our ecology, the web of life. If we go the way of the dinosaurs, then so be it, but our nature is to survive and thrive. Ultimately it is our purpose to join in union with Mother Earth. This is a quest to find or come into balance with ourselves and the natural processes, and come to understand our destiny from within our own body, heart and mind, and beyond through non-local, universal Soul consciousness.

Components of Disease

What gives healthy sustenance varies from person to person, although we do share many of the same common components in health, as we do in disease. In this list of components of disease some people are affected to a greater degree than others.

Causes of a variety of imbalances include:

- ❖ Ongoing stress — stuck in fight or flight mode
- ❖ Chronic boredom, chronic depression
- ❖ Harboring negative thoughts and emotions such as hatred, greed, jealousy, envy
- ❖ Free radical damage, oxidative stress
- ❖ Exposure to pollution, heavy metals, radiation, plastics
- ❖ Consuming foods that have been genetically modified, synthetically fertilized and sprayed with toxic pesticides
- ❖ Over-eating
- ❖ Rancid fats and oils
- ❖ A lack of wholesome saturated fats and oils
- ❖ Non-fermented soy products
- ❖ Birth control pills
- ❖ Cholesterol medication
- ❖ An excess intake of sugars, refined or raw, including fruit can cause increased insulin levels
- ❖ Refined salt containing large amounts of sodium without the other naturally occurring minerals
- ❖ Excess amounts of caffeine, alcohol and smoke
- ❖ Calcification — the intake of "bad calcium" from calcium carbonate supplements, from unfiltered or non-distilled well water and prepared foods containing hard water such as baked goods, pasta, soups, tea, coffee

- ❖ Demineralization — our soil, thus our food and our bodies have been seriously demineralized
- ❖ Over-exposure to EMFs — electro-magnetic fields
- ❖ Lack of sunshine, the use of suntan lotion and most sunscreens
- ❖ Hormonal imbalances

...the list is extensive, but above are some key examples.

Components of Health

In an onslaught of information and misinformation concerning nutrition and health, one thing is becoming obvious, there is not one diet that fits everyone. Some require a higher ratio of protein and fats and some require a higher ratio of good carbohydrates. This is why we need to be able to observe the effects that certain foods and the frequency and quantity of these foods have on our balance, as well as the effects of all other lifestyle factors. We can be our own best doctors.

Here are some universal components of health:

- ❖ Appropriate exercise, yoga, Tai Chi, stretching, meditating, whatever properly stimulates the body and quiets the mind
- ❖ Creative expression
- ❖ Sharing with others and service to humanity
- ❖ Eating organic and non-GMO food
- ❖ Eating a high percentage of raw, living foods and herbs
- ❖ Eating wholesome saturated fats and oils such as raw coconut products
- ❖ Eating super foods such as cacao, maca root, hemp seed and oil, spiralina, seaweeds, garlic and goji berries (Some should avoid all forms of sugars, for example; those with candida or cancer).
- ❖ Using super herbs such as ashwagandha, astragulus, pau d'arco, nettles, oat straw, horsetail, ginseng and turmeric
- ❖ Incorporating medicinal mushrooms such as reishi, chaga, mataki, shataki and cordiceps into the diet
- ❖ A balance of all 20 essential and non-essential amino acids

- ❖ A balance of Omega 3, 6, and 9 fatty acids, quality fish oil is a great source of omega 3, which is difficult to get enough of from a plant based diet
- ❖ Mineralization of the body through mineralization of the garden soil
- ❖ Mineralization with sea salt (such as Celtic) or rock salt (such as Himalayan)
- ❖ The appropriate amount of sunshine on one's skin providing necessary vitamin D, supplemented with vitamin D3
- ❖ Building and protecting bones with magnesium, silica and phosphorus, not from supplements containing calcium carbonate
- ❖ Maintaining healthy micro-flora or probiotics in your gut by eating fermented foods like sauerkraut and kefir
- ❖ Grounding yourself by spending time barefoot on the earth and/or utilizing grounding technology
- ❖ Controlling free radical damage

Elixir Fixer

If you are not feeling in optimum health you might try replacing one meal a day with a highly nutritious elixir, more popularly known as a smoothie. I like getting away from the term smoothie because it brings to mind a slushy, fruity drink. The idea is to make a tasty, nutritious drink that has a low sugar content, which will not raise your insulin level.

If you desire sweets you might begin with a sweeter drink and gradually cut back on the sweetener. By far, the healthiest concentrated sweetener for use in raw recipes is organic honey. You can also use blueberries or the fruit of your choice. The liquid base can be water, coconut water or your favorite tea or tea blend. You can use the more traditional fruit juice base, but that has high sugar content. Get creative and mix it up. Find the taste that pleases you.

You can get it down to an intuitive science. Study the properties and benefits of foods and herbs, and feel their effects and tweak the contents and quantities as desired. The elixir can be cold, cool or hot. It's natural to follow the seasons, cold in the summer and hot in the winter. As you get used to the taste of more bitter herbs, hot pepper and less sugar, your elixir becomes more healthful and you will tend to drink it slower which is good for digestion. And don't forget to chew your drink and drink your food.

Bob's Symbiotic Reality Elixir

*All ingredients are organic or wild crafted.

2 $^1/_2$ cups — tea made of horsetail, oat straw, nettles, pau d'arco, ground reishi mushrooms

2 heaping tablespoons — raw cacao (whole beans ground or cacao powder)

2 heaping tablespoons — hemp seeds

2 heaping tablespoons — goji berries

1 heaping tablespoons — maca root powder

1 teaspoon — spiralina

1 teaspoon — astragalus root powder

1 teaspoon — MSM (high quality sourced from trees)

1 to 2 tablespoons — extra virgin coconut oil

2 heaping tablespoons — ground sesame seeds

Cayenne and himalayan salt to taste (I like it hot)

Up to 2 cups of ice

optional ingredients: 2 tablespoons — soaked or soaked & dehydrated almonds, Brazil nuts, or walnuts, greens of choice, such as kale, spinach, parsley or wild greens

Blend until smooth (preferably in a high powered blender like a Vita Mix)

Makes 2 servings of about 12 ounces each (Usually, I like 2 servings for myself.)

Food

Let food be thy medicine
and medicine be thy food.

Hippocrates

It has been approximately 2400 years since the Hipster spoke those famous words. That was long before they hybridized the bitter medicine right out of our food, and eroded and demineralized our soils. Our pallets have been babied while our bodies have been poisoned. There is little wonder that disease runs rampant.

There is a growing movement to bring the power of food production and the security of abundant local food supplies back into the hands of the people. There is no reason for anyone to starve or even become malnourished in these times, nor is there a reason to be unemployed. There is enough gardening work to go around. The work and the benefits are good for us. Food scarcity is a myth generated by corporate interests and is rapidly becoming a self-fulfilling prophecy. Their GMO, pesticide-laden crops are failing at an unprecedented rate. There is a growing realization that corporate controlled and patented seed stock is produced merely for profit and is inferior to that of localized open pollinated and organic seeds.

Organic gardening is one of the most environmentally beneficial activities that we can do. Local, organic food is not grown with toxic pesticides, commercial fertilizers, large scale petroleum-fueled tractors, packaged in plastic and/or cardboard, shipped long distances in large fuel-guzzling trucks or refrigerated in stores and finally transported, usually in plastic and paper bags, to our homes and refrigerators.

Wasted decomposing food is a huge environmental problem due to methane and CO_2 emissions, yet uneaten homegrown food returns to compost and back to the garden.

If you have not been gardening, then join the gardening revolution and reap the nutritional and spiritual benefits. You can start a garden in your yard, join a community garden, or organize a cooperative backyard garden with neighbors and friends.

There can be as much abundance as our imagination can muster into our physical reality. It's almost infinite. It's a question of what we want to do with our land. How much concrete and asphalt do we want to cover our soil? I say the less ass-fault, the better. There's a lot of soil under that parking lot and there will be less and less cars parking on it as time goes on. Give some thought for food and some food for thought.

Vote Organic

Voting with your money effects change. What we buy we support. Buying organic, local and fair trade products have a positive impact on the environment, personal health, the health of farm workers, food packers, processors and workers involved in any agriculturally related industry. Every time you purchase organic products you are voting for a cleaner environment and healthier people.

Farm subsidies should be supporting existing organic farms and aiding in the transition from conventional to organic farms. The money can be taken directly from agricultural subsidies involving GMO and pesticide use. Organic transitioning programs allow farmers and corporate farms a reasonable period of time to make the full transition.

There will be a large increase in organic field agents. As long as a farmer meets certain criteria and shows a willingness to work with the agents, they will receive the appropriate subsidies. Fines could be put into place for those unwilling to comply, or they would simply go out of business as GMO and toxic agricultural products become unavailable. If faced with such a dilemma, most, if not all, would choose organic farming methods.

The other part of the equation is what happens to huge corporate entities like Monsanto and ADM. They must show a willingness to play fair and share the pie to be allowed to continue in existence.

The need for regulations point to design flaws. The flaws stem from the foxes guarding the hen house syndrome. It's the same old story, corporate control of our government. And, of course, that points to the hijacking of our democracy, if we ever had one.

Big money buys elections, so true campaign finance reform is extremely important in getting the corporations off our back so we can grow an organic, grass roots society. Meanwhile vote organic with your money.

Sustainable Design, Appropriate Technology and Our Ecology

When developing ideas and concepts for new designs, we can consider how it will affect the children of all species for all of time. All aspects of the human experience can now be redesigned with such considerations. We can go beyond the efficiency of a minimum negative impact to a positive impact on our ecology, which in turn will have a healing effect on our body, mind, psyche and spirit.

Corporate politicos stand in the way of this true progress. We must forge a new political reality, one that accommodates our soul revolution, and allows for eco/geographical industrial evolution, letting the renewable and replenishable resources determine a regions economic development, as we wind down our destructive economic activities.

Appropriate Technology is the perfect descriptive term in response to the madness of nuclear power, and in general, to the misdirected energy programs of the twentieth century. Appropriate, as if all life forms matter. In a compassionate society, money, or whatever form of energy exchange that is used, is a reflection of appropriate actions, not the primary consideration. What is appropriate in one location is not in another. It is dependent on what renewable resources are available in a particular region.

Along the coastlines, tidal, current, wave and wind power are perfect resources for energy generation. In the desert and dryer climates, solar and sometimes wind is appropriate. Placement of the installations becomes the primary concern. Ascetics and local environmental impact are to be considered. Appropriate technology is as localized and decentralized as possible. It also utilizes multi-functionality when possible, such as shingles that generate electricity, or "green roofs" that grow flora, filter water and help insulate the house.

The earth is a beautiful ecosystem. Everything that we need to live a healthy balanced life is here. We are of the web of life, tightly woven together like a fine thread in an exquisitely flowing blanket. Any attempt to control the Earth's resources backfires. It is collective vanity. It is collective ego. It is collective insanity. We are not above nature, or outside of nature. We are of nature, inseparable from nature. We are a tool of nature. Bringing the human experience into balance with nature and manifesting peace within ourselves and throughout humanity are of the same mission.

People's Decree

We, as citizens of the planet Earth, have the right and duty to dismantle the military-industrial complex, to put an end to war and to end all reasons for war. We have the right to eat nutritious food and drink pure water. We have the duty to make sure everyone on our planet has good food to eat and pure water to drink.

We have the right to grow our own food and save our own seeds to replant year after year. We have the right to live in a dwelling and lay claim to the rain that falls on its roof. Women have the right to manage their own reproductive system.

We have the right to maintain our own health as we see fit. We have the right to deny injections of medical drugs or vaccinations and to deny any medical procedure. We have the right to travel freely throughout the world. We have the right to practice any religion or ritual that does not restrict the freedom of anyone else or cause harm to any one being or life form.

We have the right and duty to put an end to all toxic pollution & to develop non-toxic, sustainable ways to live on our Earth. We have the right and duty to develop an economic system that is fair and equitable to all. Our duty is to end poverty and starvation, and to elevate all of the citizens of the world to an acceptable level of comfort and safety.

Peace

Peace is not merely a distant goal that we seek,
but a means by which we arrive at that goal.
Martin Luther King Jr.

We, as a civilization, have shared codependent behavior throughout his-story, patterns of being controlling or controlled, dominating or dominated. Now it is possible to alter such entrenched programming.

When aspects of nature go too far out of balance, natural corrections occur. We, being of nature, share this potential. Human nature refers to our natural instinct and natural intuition inherently available to us all. Collective human nature is a powerful force, and can be harnessed for great change. We can face our fears and our doubts and allow our primordial courage to surface and rise to the occasion.

As our higher nature evolves, and our spirit or consciousness grows, we can transform ordinary reality into a beautiful and extraordinary moment. Reconnecting with the natural processes, getting our hands in the soil and our bare feet on the earth, rediscovering herbology and natural health, remineralizing our bodies directly from the earth, harnessing natural power from the earth, sun, oceans and wind , synthesizing our vast knowledge and experience in a quest for truth and spiritual evolution are all acts of peace and direct, intentional movements away from corporate dominance, oil wars and global degradation, undermining the reasons for greed and separation.

The movement to peace requires our engagement with and alteration of the most powerful industries in the world, the military industrial complex, the medical/pharmaceutical industrial complex, the food, farming and seed industries, and the oil, coal and nuclear companies.

Militarism is the main export of the United States these days. If anything, we should be exporting photovoltaic panels, windmills, smart, hyper-efficient automobiles, and, most of all we should be exporting kindness and decency.

Divestment can be an effective tactic. Wherever we find our investments supporting dark activities, simply divest. There are plenty of attractive renewable energy stocks to divert our money to these days, as well as investment opportunities in local economies. There are new creative forms of investment opportunities unfolding in this time, such as receiving profits from energy savings through investments in appropriate energy installations, or investing in mycelium stock for mycoremediation.

Details of the solutions naturally unfold as we learn to shift into heart-based reality. As we declare peace in our hearts, we can watch people around us change and grow more peaceful by the day. Peace begins within. I can seek peace within myself and together we can nurture peaceful feelings with ourselves, like caring for tender, fragile seedlings.

Truth Seeks Its Own Level

The truth will set you free,
but first it will make you miserable.
Jim Davis

In the midst of an onslaught of mass-propaganda, there is a decentralized, unorganized, naturally evolving quest for truth and a growing desire to disseminate truth to all people. We are seeking to understand how we have been deceived and programmed in all aspects of our lives, and how to proceed from here. Light is being shed on a vast array of fallacies.

Long ago, marketing made the connection between products and our emotional weaknesses. This product will make me sexy, attractive, liked, loved, everything and anything good. The love affair with the automobile was fabricated as a deliberate attempt to end mass transit.

Materialism is like a religion to be defended, placing the importance of stuff above life.

The notion that a particular religion is the path to salvation and heaven and the rejection of that religion is the path to hell, is losing ground, yet still perpetuated to this day.

Many are under the illusion that we live in a democracy, though the corporate ties to government are becoming more obvious. The age-old belief in the necessity of war continues to be propagated. Patriotism is molded through a campaign of fear and smear tactics, separating we, "the good" from they, "the bad". Somehow people are led to believe in the opposite of truth, such as, war makes peace, GMO and the use of pesticides are safe and necessary to produce enough food to feed the world, vaccines protect us from disease, pharmaceuticals and medical procedures benefit our health, salt is bad for us and calcium supplements are good and so on. Truth lies beyond our programming.

Shift Happens

There is a huge consciousness shift occurring on our planet. Evidence of this shift can be seen in the burgeoning alternative media, in an explosion of grassroots documentaries, in a huge increase of grassroots organizations worldwide concerned with human rights and justice, and environmental issues. There is a growing interest in yoga, meditation, alternative medicines, natural healing arts and living food cuisine. An understanding of our connection to and influences on the vast web of life is rapidly unfolding.

More people every day are coming to the realization that our intentions matter, we can manifest our dreams into reality, and if we fall prey to the fear mongering, giving way to hatred, then our energy is no longer supporting peaceful change.

If you focus on the darkness, it's so hard to believe in light. The corporate media knows all too well that truth leads to change, to the dismantling of the status quo. It has become our job to take back the media and spread the truth. The truth is that wars tend to be fought for profit and resources, such as oil and real estate, for the control of human labor and /or the prevention of the spread of democracy and nationalism.

The old school corporate mentality suppresses innovative solutions to our problems, supposedly to protect their bottom line. Eventually this old school of thought will backfire.

The smart money is moving toward the development of appropriate technologies utilizing the energy from solar, wind, non-edible biofuels, tides, waves, currents, geo and ocean thermal and transitioning to organic, sustainable agriculture and healthy ways.

It's moving away from oil, coal, nuclear, bombs, death and destruction. There will be more and more liability involved with environmental destruction and crimes against humanity.

The war on terrorism is yet another excuse to profit from death and destruction. Drone attacks and manned attacks on villages can only fuel resentment, hatred and an increase in insurgencies, perpetuating destructive cycles.

To facilitate this shift we can start treating the people of the world with respect, and end our devastating policies that leave a wake of environmental destruction, poverty and starvation behind. As a growing number of us give support to such grassroots efforts, these out of control policies that maximize profits with a complete disregard for life, can be reined in and we can allow our purpose to unfold.

From Predator/Prey Syndrome To Symbiotic Reality

In the old economic paradigm, the predator or oppressor mentality has its prey or oppressed counterpart believe in scarcity and false, limiting belief systems, not in expansiveness and unlimited potential. One might be led to believe that toxic pollution and ill health is the price we must pay to live in a modern society.

This is a state of mind, as is the notion of economic depression and recession. This state is fueled by greed, a desire for material acquisition, requiring denial of our oneness of spirit and symbiotic reality, and a disregard of the connectedness and interdependence of all life.

The old school economy, which is rapidly falling apart, relies on the Predator/Prey Syndrome, rewarding the powers to be with vast fortunes for exploiting human, plant and animal resources, at a non-renewable rate.

The Predator/Prey Syndrome came from the animal world. It is obsolete in a consciously evolving society. Our spirit demands an acceptance of our oneness, of the responsibility for each other as family members.

In the new economic paradigm, economic strategies involve an intelligent master plan, utilizing the renewable resources of a local and regional area to meet the needs and desires of its people with complete regard for the entire web of life. Renewable resources refer to the naturally occurring and potentially available resources, as well as human resources or our human labor pool, regenerative, not expendable or exploitable.

In this new paradigm, educational and vocational training and retraining becomes available to all. We can look to European models for guidance.

Transportation systems will integrate bicycling and walking trails, light rail, accommodating non-edible bio-fueled and electric powered cars, taxis and distribution vehicles. Not unlike our towns and cities of today, these community centers would include vehicle stations, bus and rail stops, as well as centers for living quarters, educational facilities, markets, shops, restaurants, entertainment venues and community gardens. These centers would be intertwined and surrounded by wilderness and farms, as well as wilderness farms, a merging, a blending, a reunion.

Vehicle battery swap stations provide a quick exchange for electric vehicles where spent batteries are traded for recharged ones. Charging stations utilize the appropriate energy source for a particular region — solar, wind, geo thermal, ocean thermal, tidal, and/or various combinations.

These swap stations exist today. We are in the midst of an *E Volution* (electric vehicle revolution) as well as a movement toward cars on demand. Many will opt out of car ownership all together.

The main distinctions between conventional city centers and these future community centers will be that the air and the waterways will be clean, for all energy sources will be non-toxic, all runoff and waste water will be dealt with in a symbiotic manner, and these centers will naturally and aesthetically flow with human nature, emphasizing public transportation, walking and bicycling. Natural, ascetic and edible landscape will flow throughout our symbiotic reality.

Paradigms

A paradigm is a pattern or a model, a set of assumptions, concepts, values and practices that constitutes a way of viewing reality.

Old Paradigms	New Paradigms
Waging war Starvation Degradation	Spreading peace Nurturing life
Using nature & her resources for our personal gain	Being a tool of nature. Realizing we are of nature.
Racism, Ageism, Sexism, Classism, Religionism, foodism, denial	Oneness Equality Justice Acceptance
Corporate power exploits the human workforce and natural resources. Trans-national corporate economies, based on greed.	Power transfer to the people. Corporations serve the human population. Local, grassroots economies, rooted in community.
Stagnant, ego-based conceptual thought	Expanding consciousness
Cynicism	Optimism
Petroleum based combustion engines	EVs (electric vehicles)
Coal, Oil, Nukes, Gas	Solar, Wind, Geo-thermal Ocean-thermal, Tidal power, current power, wave power, Non-edible bio-fuels
Petroleum based, corporate controlled agriculture	Organic, sustainable, community and family based agriculture
Chlorinated plastics Toxic synthetic fibers Heavy metal dyes and inks	Non-toxic polymers Natural fibers including hemp Natural dyes and inks

A Chain of Acquaintances

The theory "six degrees of separation" states that any person on Earth is connected to any other person through a chain of acquaintances of no more than six people. There is at least an element of truth to this theory. Even if it is off by two or three people, it is still such a phenomenal concept. It states how connected we are as a civilization, and how quickly we can spread positive reality throughout the world, if we so choose.

Solutions Abound

There is no shortage of visions or solutions. The dams, holding back the solutions, are breaching from the shear expansion of consciousness. The beautiful ideas and technologies are springing forth, levitating to the occasion from the earthen energy, brimming and collecting in streams of gratitude and understanding. Opportunities abound. We can work together in a cooperative manner, allowing all to be involved and prosper.

Whether we know it or not, we all want to share in soul purpose, and be the collective solution. It no longer needs to be about competition and exclusion. We are in the midst of a soul revolution, of conscious evolution. Evoke the inner flower child deep inside. We can move beyond our karma, through works of love and kindness, to join the greater collective consciousness.

Money and Life's Schisms

If we follow the path to money for money's sake, we have strayed from our passionate expression. It is easy to fall into such a quandary. It is best to catch people when they are very young and help them realize their creative inclinations and nurture their creative passion. For those of us who have fallen into to life's schisms, that chasm between one's passion and one's quest for money or monetary stability can be ever widening.

The path back to independence from servitude can be a steep uphill struggle. There is no one simple answer. Or, is the answer simply to approach each moment as a ride floating downstream? Is it our resistance to *what is* that causes most of our dis-ease, and renders us seemingly helpless in changing what is?

If you develop your creative skills early in life, your chance of marrying your life's passion with financial success is much greater than later in life. But it's never too late. I released my first musical album at the age of 57, and my second album at 59. I began *Meanderings in Symbiotic Reality*, my first book, at the age of 58. For some of us, it takes a while to realize the power of intention, the reality of synchronicity, the ease of following one's passion, and the outpouring of creativity that follows. It helps to banish negative belief patterns from our programming.

To jump into the stream of creative flow is to be in a timeless reality that has always existed, no beginning and no ending. It just IS. It doesn't matter when we have arrived, in essence, we have always been there.

Finding Our Bearings

Our internal compass can always point to truth, like true north. Awareness, knowledge and perception of natural/universal reality, is the magnetic force. We on planet Earth have not been living according to the universal or natural plan, at least not as a societal entity. Look at the symbiosis of forest life. That is nature's plan. We can recalibrate our internal compass to the natural rhythms and symbiotic reality. The recalibration is under way.

Positive Change Can Happen

All one needs to do is look back to the transitional period of post-World War II. McCarthyism and the J. Edgar Hoover mentality was wreaking havoc on the freedoms in our society in the 1950's and into the 1960's, with their tactics of blacklisting communist sympathizers, of FBI surveillance, interference and infiltration of activist organizations, of intimidation, jailing and even murder of union organizers, civil rights leaders, anti-war activists or anyone who publicly made a stand for human rights and freedoms.

In response to such a fascist assault on our freedoms, the "60's generation" rose up and forced an end to the Vietnam war, made great strides in civil rights, women's rights, gay rights, organic gardening and farming, alternative technologies, healing arts, political activism, experimentation in community structures and grass roots organizing, and in general became more eclectic and open minded in regard to philosophy, religion and spirit.

By the time 1975 had arrived, a most unusual revolution had radically altered our reality. At that point, the political conservatives rolled up their sleeves and went to work, swearing never again will they let a bunch of hippies and liberal politicos sidetrack plans for their new world order. From their perspective they have done quite well. It has been said that we won the revolution and went back to the bars and got drunk. Certainly good works have occurred since the 70's, strides have been made, but much ground has been lost to the corporate fundamentalists. However, we are now paralleling those tumultuous times. One can only speculate on the outcome, but as the bad gets worse, positive change is occurring at an ever-increasing rate.

People around the world are fed up with the old corporate and militant dominance mentality. In January of 2011, one man who was barely supporting his family by selling fruit on the streets of Tunisia was shut down over a licensing issue. He was assaulted and humiliated by the police during the incident. Unable to cope with his situation anymore, he lit himself on fire.

Like a fuse, he unknowingly ignited an uprising in his country, forcing the dictator of 32 years to flee. As popular uprisings spread throughout the region, 18 days of protests forced Hosni Mubarak, Egypt's dictatorial president to step down. Such hope for self-determination has not been felt in the Arab world for generations. Time will tell the story, but we know what people want, the freedom to live, prosper, and care for each other and for our beautiful world.

Bet on Your Highest Aspirations to Win

In the meditative state, a connection to our universal reality can occur, offering a glimpse into natural order or balance. From such order we know anything is possible. What is out of balance can be balanced, minds can change and universal realty can be collectively perceived. The great theory of our times is that there is a point of awakening collectively to universal consciousness when the scales are tipped and the glorious work towards peace, justice, betterment of the human experience and compassion for all life will become our global reality.

A growing number of us choose to sing songs of peace, paint pictures of beauty, and keep our eyes on truth and our souls resting in utopian dreams. That is not a dichotomy. Forms of non-reality and mental imbalance arise when we harbor attachments to utopian dreams and we shade the truth to suit our fragile minds.

Cynicism is the other side of that same coin. The future outcome is speculative. The human experience may be required to go the way of the dinosaur. The truth is we just don't know. We cannot be attached to the future. That is unrealistic. We can only live now, in a continuation of present moments. Life is rather momentary. There is no time like the present. Though, when speculating on the future, why not place our faith on our highest aspirations?

There is No Time Like the Present

In essence there is no time. There is earth time, relating to our 24-hour day, a full spin on its axis. There is earth/sun time, measuring earth's trip around the sun. But if we back away from the earth and sun, then *is there time*? Time becomes nothing more than a continual collection of present moments, and not even that if there is no one around to acknowledge the momentary fragments of mental perception. Timeless flow just is.

When we slide into the zone via meditation or through passionate pursuit, we have entered this flow, albeit momentarily. In western thought our moments are chopped up into so many nonsensical fragments. It is quite a science, each second ticking its way to a new minute, hour, day, week, month, year, fairly accurately.

The ancient indigenous people lived in a natural time zone or non-time zone. They did not need a clock to tell them when the sun's light would come and go, and when the seasons would cycle. Intuitive powers are heightened when living with nature. There is no mystery that the earth is a sphere spinning around the sun, an idea that apparently evaded some in western thought, or at least so we are told. Concepts of time run contrary to timeless flow. It's like the ego trying to define spirit.

Time?
It's Always Now

*Realize deeply that the present moment
is all you ever have.*

Eckhart Tolle

Now is when we change reality. Mental yearnings to alter our past can reside in our subconscious until we give in to the present and no longer resist *what is*. The letting go, the non-attachment, is what allows the space for change to unfold. Clearing the mind and forever beginning anew, with a blank canvas, allows us to see the creative possibilities.

Altering the landscape of reality is an art form. Sculpting rigid mindsets into flexible, malleable, open perspectives requires poignant expressions of the arts; poetry, spoken word, music, visual arts, documentaries, utopian fictions, all of the art forms. Perhaps one of the most important art forms is one to one human connection, touching individual hearts, pointing to hope through reason and spreading infectious kindness.

Beyond Good and Evil?

The dualism of good and evil within humanity has unfolded in a scenario of imperialistic dominance clashing and subsiding with an evolving indigenous and collective conscious reality. A continual ebb and flow of waves and undertow are pulling on each other. Are we evolving? Perhaps we have had to endure such barbarism, such brutal inequities for so long, for the road from animalistic survival to evolved spiritual beings is a long, arduous journey, yet seemingly inevitable. It is a great leap from survival of the fittest to a collective realization of oneness and love consciousness.

Imagine where we would be with that aggressive energy channeled into spirited pursuits. Perhaps concepts of dualism will give way to the collective realization of our connectedness to the all-encompassing universal reality.

Cooperative Compassionate Enterprise

When mentioning ideas of using our tax money to insure basic rights and comforts to all of our citizens, the typical American programmed response is, “that sounds like socialism,” most often spoken in a derogatory manner. Those responsible for spinning socialism into a four-letter word are also the individuals who support huge subsidies for corporations, known as corporate socialism or corporate welfare.

Socialism is a dying word. So be it. Why fight the fundamentalist think-tankers. Best out think them. The beauty is that we have decency and compassion on our side, which is much more convincing than greed and hatred.

Like mortal bodies, all isms are bound to pass away. Any good, descriptive term can and will eventually be perverted. We need to keep the terminology one step ahead of the game. Play around. Someone comes up with the catchy terms and phrases of the day, why can’t it be you and me? Here are some ideas: Compassionism, Loveservatism, Kindservatism, Compassionative, Loveservative, Kindservative, the Love System, Love First, Love over Politics, Love not Politrix, the Party of One.

The Coffee Party is a response to the divisive, right wing Tea Party. Listen, for solutions are told as problems unfold.

Some northern European countries employ systems that protect people from job loss, home foreclosures, medical bankruptcies and the like. Some are referring to such systems as social capitalism.

The “Bulivarian Revolution” is sweeping South America, bringing to power socialist leaders who are implementing much beneficial change for the people. Contrary to US mass media propaganda, which is a campaign of lies and deceit, leaders such as Hugo Chavez, president of Venezuela, and Evo Morales, president of Bolivia, are greatly reducing poverty, reclaiming water rights and oil rights from international corporations and allowing profits to benefit the people. They are affording universal health care. Small business ownership is becoming increasingly available to the people.

No matter how you spell it, it's time to move beyond corporate capitalism and centralized power structures. Let's overthrow our corporate sponsored government, elect people for the people, develop eco-regional economies, and adopt a 100% employment strategy paying living wages that brings forth a prosperous, sustainable society.

Eliminate corporate welfare and allow appropriate economies to develop. With a combination of private sector and government sector funding, sustainable job training can become an option for a large percentage of our unemployed, paying at least a minimum wage during the training period. The public and private sectors could benefit greatly from nurturing a skilled, up to date, green work force.

No matter what spins are put on the terminology of the day, we all know what compassion means and most of us know that is a good thing. Live up, live right, support what is good and withdraw support from what is not.

Natural Reality

Departure from natural reality is typically the fundamental cause of dis-ease. Sit by a river, listen to the flowing water, feel the breeze, see the sun filtering through the leaves as the shadows dance with the dragonflies. Surrender to the healing powers of nature's meditative reality. Answers emerge in such a state.

Human nature is of nature. Collective human nature can be a powerful force. Face your fear, engage your fear and you may, at least momentarily, experience fearlessness. Engage your naturalness while flowing with your emotional waves and you can transform ordinary reality into a beautiful and extraordinary moment.

Love and Kindness

Love and kindness is as natural for humans as collecting and spreading pollen is for bees. It feeds on itself. It gains strength in collective consciousness. It builds trust. It is soul purpose manifesting in reality, from the ethereal to the physical. Beyond survival, it is our reason for living. That which allows love to grow is our soul purpose.

From the Source Springs Truth

Can we trust our mind? Can we trust our feelings? Can we delve within our interior to find the answers? We would have to journey through our subconscious and explore our programming in order to understand the habitual patterns of the mind. We would have to hold eternal vigilance, for the trickster ego just loves to jump behind the wheel and steer us in its own direction, allowing for irrational thought. That is how we can do what we do to people, to ourselves and to the world, without consciously feeling guilt.

The mind can serve as a beautiful component. When we are centered in love, in soul, the explorative and imaginative mind can come to profound understanding and can help to perceive what is. Can we agree on certain premises to base our thoughts and feelings on? If we can quiet our mind long enough to perceive reality through our soul, we can lay a strong and pure foundation to build a new reality upon.

These premises might include such basics as:

- ❖ Life is one universal entity.
- ❖ Harm any part of it and we harm ourselves.
- ❖ We do not wish to harm ourselves.
- ❖ We care for our natural world and we don't want to destroy it.
- ❖ Our physical and mental perceptions barely scratch the surface of infinite reality and infinite possibilities.
- ❖ It is okay to be a humble speck in the vast cosmos.
- ❖ We respect all people, all life.
- ❖ We don't want to cause unneeded pain and suffering.
- ❖ We want health, happiness, prosperity and longevity for ourselves and our children.
- ❖ Our neighbors want the same, as do their neighbors, as do those throughout the whole world.

- ❖ Wishing to change the past, is to live in non-reality.
- ❖ We can change in the now, but what is done is done.
- ❖ Blame brings only pain.

Like altering our diet, when changing our mind's diet, it is suggested to add in what is palatable, and allow the negative thinking to atrophy from a lack of use. There is no reason to force yourself to believe we are all one, if you don't. There can always be an alternative route. It may be that through embracing respect for all life, a feeling of connectedness or oneness may arise in time.

However, philosophical differences, like religious differences, are unimportant. It is the reverence for life and the nurturing of life that is important. Add in what feels right and real, and allow ourselves to evolve. Higher states of awareness will be inevitable, as well as unavoidable. Nothing is stagnant. In the vast timeless, universal flow, everything changes, always.

93,000,000 Miles is Close Enough for Comfort

The smartest, most efficient energy production is small scale and decentralized, like neighborhood wind generators and solar collectors, right at the source of your needs. For your hot water, heat the water on your roof within 10 or 20 feet of your existing plumbing.

Nuclear energy was a lie from the beginning. They just had to try out their new toy and kill hundreds of thousands of people in Hiroshima and Nagasaki, even when they knew the war was coming to an end.

In the 1950's, nuclear energy was marketed as clean, cheap and safe. There is nothing clean, cheap or safe about mining uranium, about generating, transporting and storing radioactive waste, about reactor malfunctions and nuclear meltdowns, like Three Mile Island, Chernobyl and Fukushima. The idea of nuclear war is born of the darkest minds of our times. It was a lie. It is still a lie. It has always been about nuclear weapons, big bucks, big power and world domination strategies.

We need nuclear power and we need to keep it 93,000,000 miles from Earth. The lies have continued, probably from time immemorial. They are so good at it, and getting better. So good, in fact, that bad is great.

Corporate, Elitist and Governmental politics are beyond the absurd, far beyond the realm of rational or logical thought and worlds apart from natural intuitive reality. It is a horribly bizarre movie that seems to have no end.

Let's fire the writers, the producers and all of the crew, and immediately begin production on Harvey Wasserman's *Solartopia*. In this Utopian fiction the location of the movie is the entire world, and the fiction is a scenario for reality. What Harvey refers to as King CONG (coal, oil, nuclear, gas), is outlawed worldwide and everything reasonable under the sun is implemented, from technologies that exist to those that are within our grasp.

We now know our physical reality begins in our imagination and in our dreams, then nurtured as intentions, brought into conceptual reality, disseminated into our collective consciousness, and finally manifested into our physical reality. Each one of us has unlimited potential in this respect. I urge you to read *Solartopia* and allow this beautiful scenario to live within our collective vision.

Mycelium, Humans and the Internet

I see the mycelium as the
Earth's natural Internet.....

The mycelium stays in constant molecular communication with its environment, devising diverse enzymatic and chemical responses to complex challenges.

Paul Stamets

A mycelial mat is an intelligent entity. Having similar ancestral roots as fungi, humans are also intelligent entities at the molecular level. The human body is a vast network of constant, inter connected, cellular communication. As human collective consciousness evolves, so does our inter-societal communication, facilitated by worldwide connections of individuals through the internet.

We are a collective entity getting to know our self. The internet's spontaneous, multi-level, mass communicative structure mimics a mycelial web. There is little doubt that the human network is designed to communicate with itself as well as with its surrounding ecosystem without external technologies. It's a stretch of the imagination to visualize such a connection between fungi, humans and the internet, but as we delve deeper into the fascinating world of mycelium, and as we exercise such intuitive ponderings, it begins to make complete sense. It should become common knowledge that what connects individual human vessels to each other is similar to a fungal web, not visible to the eye, yet perceptible nonetheless.

The separation of the physical and the metaphysical is conceptual, yet another way that the mind divides our one whole reality into separate compartments. In an attempt to understand so many aspects of life, does the mind tend to lead us astray? Is what we perceive reality, or is our perception barely scratching the surface of reality?

Mycelium offers great hope in toxic remediation. Humans can spend hundreds of years trying to come to terms with certain truths, while a mycelial mat communicates pure intelligence, sending instant signals alerting itself of alien toxicity and going into immediate action.

What Can We Do?

Plant a garden. Shop in local food co-ops. Support local farmers, crafts people, artists and musicians at farmers markets and festivals. We can build social movements, and form or join local, grassroots groups that rally around common causes. We, as citizens, can engage with our elected leaders, and be so many thorns in the politicians' sides. We can develop ideas and make policy proposals and recommendations.

We, the people, create democracy, not the politicians. We can be a part of our community radio and TV stations. Free speech begins with individuals speaking freely and honestly. Listen to what you say. Do you mean what you say? Do you say what you feel? The more I write these words, the more I realize what I believe and how to better communicate how I feel. We can learn the art of debate, the art of speaking, as well as the art of listening.

Organize for positive Earth changes. Support appropriate technologies (solar, wind, etc.). Organize against destructive practices of industry and militant actions. Know the truth. Go mass media free or find the appropriate community and grass roots news sources that you can trust. If a station or network is sponsored by large destructive corporations, you can bet they are influencing or compromising the journalistic integrity of the newscasts. Use your intelligence. Always "question authority." Keep cynicism at bay, for, if we allow it to fester and grow in our consciousness, our sense of truth will be compromised.

Knowing the truth and collectively acting on it, as decent world citizens in the know would do, is the finest medicine for an ill society. Answers abound. Collective focus, intention and resolve just need some development. We can place the value of all people and of all life above cheap, available products. Life is precious. Product is stuff.

Enjoy life. Sing. Dance. Share your food. Share your ideas. Allow others to share with you. Plant seeds literally and metaphorically. Open to the harsh truths and realities imposed by militant governments on its own people and by imperialistic, corporate and governmental entities.

This is the beginning movement toward change that can positively affect our global community. It is not possible to block out such realities. We are affected, whether we know it or not, by the vibrations of destruction of our natural world and by government sponsored mass murder, degradation, and impoverishment of segments of our world population. It's our collective karma that we can't avoid.

The richest of the rich is as poor as the poorest of spirit, unless constant and tireless action is taken to heal the earth and its' inhabitants. We are nourished by our own actions and collectively nourished by our collective actions of sharing and kindness.

Take some time for yourself. Fast, drink pure water, breath clean air and meditate in nature. Contemplate the trees, clouds and creeks. Ask the universe to connect with you in a partnership. Seek truth and purpose, for you and for all. Ponder the shift. What does it mean? What can I do? What can we do? Share your waking and dreaming vibrations with the healing process.

Withdraw your attention from energies that no longer serve you or the greater good. Allow your desire for decadence to subside. Add in the good stuff and let the negative influences fade away naturally. Let go of guilt. Allow your evolution and your connection to our collective evolution to unfold naturally in present time. Remember present time is all we really have. The mind harbors illusions of past and future time, but reality only occurs in the now. Doubt feeds doubt. If you believe you can't, then you are correct. There is no purpose in spending time in doubt.

Go for the highest of possibilities. Go for the positive. It can only be better than what comes from doubting yourself. When you feel we are interring realms of "Heaven" or Spirit Manifest, we just may be. Simultaneous events can occur. Where our attention goes, such energy grows. Fast from TV and listen to nature. Do it until you no longer desire the drug-ness of TV. You don't have to quit anything. Your wise self will merely let go of what it no longer desires.

Gather with friends and family. Get some drums and find a rhythm. Don't be shy and don't worry about you or anyone being off beat. It's a process of letting go of the ego and excessive mental activity. Keep drumming, find the beat and feel the vibration in your heart. The group will help heart to open and the rhythm to resonate with earth vibrations. Keep drumming with your people. You will begin to feel your tribal connectedness with your fellow drummers and with life vibrations beyond your circle. Feel the oneness of all people and all life forms, one planetary experience, one universal experience.

Ask yourself, am I invested in destructive companies or war profiteers? Is that what I want, or do I want abundance for our oneness? How do I invest in beauty? There are non-conventional ways to invest, such as cost savings investments from weatherizing your house, installing solar collectors on your roof, solar screens, etc. The paybacks and future savings can be calculated and can be just as real as making interest on a conventional investment.

Discovering our emotional history can help us heal our greater self. The very way we carry and hold our body, the way we breathe, deeply or barely, stems from our emotional background, from our impressionable days as a child. There is a wide range of techniques for understanding our emotional makeup and letting go of past emotional stresses and traumas. There are quite a variety of therapies, body /mind and body/energy therapies. One can develop the ability to look within oneself and view the emotional terrain honestly.

If needed, the right technique and therapist will likely come into view. The body, mind and emotional healing process may not require money to procure professional help, but will require the desire to understand one's inner workings and time to read works from inspiring writers, delve into meditation, yoga, long walks in nature, fasting, adding in organic and wild living foods to one's diet and reconnect with our Earth Mother. Lie in the grass and walk barefoot on the Earth..

We Are All In This Together

We all have a role to play, our individual and collective destiny to fulfill. We have freewill. We have choices, and as we choose, our destiny unfolds. This revolution is for everyone and against no one.

The adversary is darkness itself, hatred, terror, servitude and slavery, sexism, ageism, racism, classism, militarism, war, suffering, dis-ease, doubt and fear.

The goal is to shed light on all dark aspects of human existence and to pave the way to a beautiful, compassionate way of living together on our planet.

The Time Has Come

The time has come for us to see
The time has come for us to be
The ones to rise above
And heal our world with love

Too many live in illusion
Every day and every night
Resounding the confusion
Stripped of our natural rights

Let us pray for the waking day
When we realize life is for loving
We'll eliminate the weapons of hate
And see that love is for living

Can human destination be world salvation?
When the excavation of love is so deep
Can human realization rise to the occasion?
Can we wake up from our sleep?

In this time of need and greed
Can we find the right equation?
If those who know will plant the seeds
And to all deliver love's invitation

"The Time Has Come" is a song written by Bob SLaughter.
It appears on the album *"Bob Here Now."*

Love's Invitation

Love's invitation to all the people of the world vs. business-as-usual is our choice at this juncture. Delivering this invitation, of course, means a restructuring of most activities on earth. Huge opportunities abound. They are of a different nature. No less than a melding of the brilliance of the western mind with the spirit and connectedness to the earth of the ancient indigenous peoples.

Certainly a sense of personal stability and security would increase for most of us, but for the ultra-rich, a wealth of gratification would overcome the habitual greed that prevails in this capitalistic climate.

To invite love into the world means an immediate departure from toxic activities, and a complete movement towards clean, green construction, energy and agriculture.

Love is non-exclusive and all-inclusive. It includes compassion for all life, so harm to any life form through industrial activities is not acceptable. Every step of the way opens up new opportunities for employment, for creative solutions to replace old destructive ways.

It Ebbs, It Flows, It Slows, It Grows

To be conscious is to be aware, to know. Awareness is consciousness. It is invisible, but we know it exists. Whether experienced by one or a million it is still real. It can offer a glimpse into potential reality.

It grows and subsides. It can be still and quiet like a meditation, and it can stir truth to passionate action. Consciousness can grow to tidal wave proportions and flood reality. It has happened before and it will happen again.

"Yellow Submarine" was one of those great works that epitomized the hippy revolution.

"Yes" became the theme of the day. "No" was changed to "know." The blue meanies represented intolerance, oppression and blind injustice. Pepperland was conscious reality manifest.

If you are around 60, give or take a few years, it is likely that to some extent you experienced such collective optimism. We, of the counter culture, felt empowered and hopeful, if not cocky. The Vietnam War was shut down. Nixon and Agnew were forced from office. Environmental radicalism was taking hold. We were building solidarity with Native Americans. There was a back to the land boom. Intentional communities sprang up across the country, as well as housing coops and food coops. We built solar collectors and wind mills, became organic gardeners and farmers, developed permaculture, experimented with a vast array of diets and healing practices, drawing from ancient cultures and making it up along the way. We aspired to non-consumerism and self-sufficiency.

For the earthy, organic types, the 70's were a beautiful time. For the materialistic at heart, the 80's and Reagan's gang brought great opportunities, while spelling the beginning of the decline of the working class, and taking aim at the heart of the counterculture that had been a thorn in their side for the last couple of decades. "Nancy's War on Drugs" was a war on their own country's people — us.

In this new Reaganomics mentality, greed had been deregulated and human life had been devalued. The dharma bums and the hitchhiking hippies started looking like street people, more in their expression of despair than their long hair and dirty clothes. All of this was our-story of America. The true stories from the "world of color" are best told by those who experienced them first hand. They are stories of horrible and ridiculous acts of government and elitist sponsored police brutality, to the more "humane" gentrification of entire neighborhoods, a kind of clinical or sophisticated ethnic cleansing, reality truly beyond my description, stemming from the days of the conquerors, through the days of slavery, to present day where you can find it all right here in "America." It has never been so bad, and it has never been so good.

These days we are fortunate to have a wealth of wisdom in the aging 60's generation and a courageous revolutionary spirit in the young and the young at heart. It takes youth to point to the absurdities that the more experienced have grown accustomed to, or at least have accepted as inevitable. All that is inevitable is the ebb and flow of consciousness.

Evoke the Revolutionary Spirit

...... of Abbey Hoffman and the Yippies, the genius intellect of Frank Zappa, the piercing comedic honesty of Lord Buckley, Paul Krasner, Lenny Bruce, George Carlin and Bill Hicks.

Draw from the creative spirit of Ken Kesey and the Merry Pranksters, and the clowns of protest, the clowns of soul, from Wavy Gravy to the Mexican clowns of journalism, the unleashed journalistic wildness of Hunter S. Thompson, the beat poetry of Alan Ginsberg and William Burroughs.

Learn from their artistic tactics of Guerilla Theater. See the power of pure intentions turned to heartfelt actions through those like Mother Teresa and today's Greg Mortenson, and so many on the ground that never become famous.

Feel the inspiration of musical genius in Louis Armstrong, Miles Davis, Bob Marley and John Lennon. Music communicates with or without words. Know the lineage of non-violent activism, from the works of Henry David Thoreau to Gandhi to Nelson Mandela to Martin Luther King Jr, the artistic descent of Charlie Chaplin, and the revolutionary genius of Thomas Jefferson.

Study the lives of Che Guevera, Fidel Castro and the Bulivarian revolutionaries of today; Hugo Chavez and Evo Morales.

Come to your own conclusions as to the value of resistance to an uncaring, capitalistic machine that will bulldoze love, decency, kindness and compassion, and literally bulldoze old growth forests, ancient olive groves, entire eco systems, as well as any human beings that stand in the way of their "progress".

Learn our "history." To study US "history" is to study world "history," for the brutal mentality of the western movement of man, from the days of Columbus to modern day capitalism, has spread like a virus, infecting all corners of the world.

Understand what happened to our money from the 1800's to 1913 to present day. Know the CIA's involvement in military coups and the destabilizing of governments throughout the world, so many

Latin American countries, Middle Eastern countries, newly formed, democratically elected governments smashed by US backed juntas.

Know that this continues into the 21st century, in countries such as Honduras and Haiti. Find out why billions of dollars of donations for Haiti relief sits in bank accounts, unavailable to the hundreds of thousands of Haitians living in the mud and dying of cholera.

See that Palestinians live in a prison called Gaza, and Iraqis breathe depleted uranium from US bombs. We owe it to the world to learn the truth, in order to make amends.

When we begin to mend our ways and reach out to the world, we can forgive ourselves, from those of us on the front lines of war, to those of us who passively shudder at the thought of the atrocities committed by our leaders and fueled by our tax dollars. There is no excuse for complicity.

Thanks to the tax resisters, the dissenters, the Julian Assanges and the Bradley Mannings of the world, the Yes Men, the twisters of the spinners, those who speak truth to power and risk imprisonment and death, to all of the everyday people who care and knowingly share in our extraordinary spirit, and zeal for life, for cultural roots, who respect each other and our differences.

Our power grows with our collective intelligence. May we never forget that our quest is for truth; our job description is janitors of karma, doctors of soul and sculptors of happiness. Our mission is peace on earth and food, clothing and shelter for all.

Affirmations for a New World

Humanity is a collective organism. We as a collective entity recognize the futility of our destructive behavior. Coming back into alignment with universal flow, offers such exciting prospects, enticing everyone, including the very rich, to become involved.

We rise every day, energized with the thought of a new day's agenda. "It's another beautiful day on earth. We heal the earth today." Everyone is included, from hundredaires to billionaires. It's an inclusive approach that is moving us into a new paradigm of soul consciousness, of peace and mutual prosperity on earth, removing the reason, the will and the desire for war and terrorism.

We are waging peace and kindness with our world of people. We are shifting our economies from fighting disease to nurturing health, removing toxins from our environment, and creating a positive environmental impact, growing oxygen and emitting clean water.

The messages of peace, love, understanding, justice, flowing, sustainable economies, organic living foods, health and healing are spreading across our globe. We are spreading these messages through our music, poetry, art, sharing of our love, wisdom and experience. GMO poisoned foods are abandoned. Dams are breached. *Solartopia* is becoming our new reality. We are with nature. We are evolving technologies in harmony with the natural world. Stagnant conceptions and darkness of the body, heart, mind and soul fade away. We awaken to the glorious wonder. We open to love consciousness.

Explore the Realms of Possibilities

Thanks for meandering through these pages with me. It doesn't matter if you agree with everything that I wrote here. I'm not sure I do. I just hope I stimulated some ideas.

We all have our own inclinations, our own approaches to life. Some are more nurturing, some are more revolutionary, some are healers, or messengers, or researchers, or programmers, some are artists, others love to garden, some are designers and some are constructors. It matters not what you love to do, rather what you do with what you love. Can you make it work for you? Can you weave your life, your work into symbiotic reality?

My challenge to you and me is to arise each morning and cultivate an attitude of optimism. Reality is our garden to grow what we wish. Apply creativity to what lies in front of us. We are the artists and the world is our canvas. What seem to be problems and setbacks may actually offer understanding and build strength. We can dream of grandiose ideas, realize our power within, and together we can turn beautiful ideas into reality.

I will leave you with an example of a homegrown idea, a Utopian fiction that could become reality, and is written as if it will. It is an idea that unfolded as I was writing this book and writing and recording my new album "It's Just a Ride".

> As I imagined what postmodern, symbiotic reality would look like, it made perfect sense that EVs would play a huge role in the unfolding of that eco-reality. I had read somewhere, perhaps in *Solartopia*, about battery exchange stations and incorporated the idea into my book.
>
> Then I came across an article about a man who had envisioned a way to end our need for gasoline by developing a network of battery swap stations that could change out a car's power source, a large flat battery underneath the car, in approximately one minute, automatically with robotics, offering a continual driving experience. Charging stations could be conveniently located for topping up a car's battery when not in use.

This man found the needed venture capital, developed a highly skilled team, formed a battery and swap station company, partnered with major car companies, and is in the process of bringing his ideas into reality. I, of course, love this idea and want to become involved in promoting plans for swap stations in Texas, and up the I-35 corridor to Minneapolis, while touring my book and album in an electric car.

"It's Just a Ride" took on a whole new meaning. On the cover of the album, I sit in a new electric car shooting the peace sign, because that's what it is really about— peace and natural balance. EVs, windmills and solar panels are stepping stones leading us in that direction.

While stopping and charging, I will promote EVs, showing the need for an infrastructure of battery swap and charging stations.

A film will document the entire process, the coordination of sponsorships with the car company and the acquisition of a new EV, and with one or more hotel chains that would set up charging stations and provide battery charging and lodging along a network of stops no more than 100 miles apart, a safe distance between charges.

At each stop, gigs and book signing events will be lined up, along with TV and radio spots to promote the battery swap and charging stations. I will interview executives of the sponsoring companies, clarifying our common goals.

The documentary culminates with a symbiotic reality festival and a performance of songs from "It's Just a Ride" in Austin, Texas, the heart of Texas' politics, the capital of live music, and the land of progressive action.

Dream splendid, grandiose, beautiful dreams.
Develop intelligent, creative, coherent plans.
Seek out mutually beneficial partnerships.
Bring your dreams to fruition
with good old diligent, hard work.
May you live a long, prosperous,
healthy and happy life.

Namaste

Resources

Journalism and Activism

KPFA – Pacifica, Free Speech Radio
http://www.kpfa.org/

Flashpoints with Dennis Bernstein on KPFA

Livingroom and Saturday Morning Talkies with Kris Welch on KPFA

Aljazeera News
http://english.aljazeera.net/

Democracy Now with Amy Goodman
http://www.democracynow.org/

Greg Palast
http://www.gregpalast.com/

Project Censored
http://www.projectcensored.org/

Counterpunch – An Online Political Newsletter
http://www.counterpunch.org/

Truth Out
http://www.truth-out.org/

WikiLeaks
http://wikileaks.org/

Chris Hedges
http://www.truthdig.com/articles_by_author/Chris_Hedges/

Jordan Flaherty – Before & after Katrina
http://floodlines.org/

David Swanson
http://davidswanson.org/

Formerly After Downing Street
http://warisacrime.org/

Daniel Ellsberg
http://www.ellsberg.net/

David Lindorff
http://ThisCantBeHappening.net/

Kevin Annett – Focused on Canadian genocide
http://www.hiddenfromhistory.org/

Kevin Pina – Journalist focused on Haiti
http://www.haitiinformationproject.net/

Food Not Bombs
http://www.foodnotbombs.net/

The Institute for Policy Studies
http://www.ips-dc.org/

Marilyn Waring
http://marilynwaring.com/

International Affairs

Stones Into Schools by Greg Mortenson
http://www.gregmortenson.com/

The Chavez Code by Eva Golinger
http://www.chavezcode.com

South of the Border by Oliver Stone
http://southoftheborderdoc.com/

The Free Gaza Movement
http://www.freegaza.org/

Mexico Unconquered: Chronicles of Power and Revolt by John Gibler

Voices of the Middle East and North Africa
http://vomena.org/

Economics

William Black
"The Best Way to Rob a Bank Is to Own One"

Catherine Austin Fitts
http://solari.com/

Robert Reich
http://robertreich.org/
http:/robertreich.blogspot.com/

Center For Economic and Policy Research
http://www.cepr.net/

Indigenous People & Their Rights

Republic of Lakota
http://www.republicoflakotah.com/

American Indian Movement
http://www.aimovement.org/

Center for World Indigenous studies
http://cwis.org/

Hopi Cultural Preservation Office
http://www.nau.edu/~hcpo-p/

Net Neutrality Issues

Center For Media Justice
http://centerformediajustice.org/

Free Press
http://www.freepress.net/

History

Howard Zinn
http://www.howardzinn.org/default/index.php

Noam Chomsky
http://www.chomsky.info/

Moving Beyond GMO

Organic Consumers Association (OCA)
http://www.organicconsumers.org/

Jeffery Smith — Spilling the Beans
http://www.responsibletechnology.org/

Consciousness

Deepak Chopra
http://www.chopra.com/

Eckhardt Tolle
http://www.eckharttolle.com/home/

Dalai Lama
http://www.dalailama.com /

Wayne Dyer
http://www.drwaynedyer.com/

Louise Hay
http://www.louisehay.com/

Debbie Ford
http://www.debbieford.com/

Marianne Williamson
http://marianne.com/

Health

David Wolfe
http://www.davidwolfe.com

Dr. Joseph Mercola
http://www.mercola.com/

Donna Gates
http://www.bodyecology.com/

John Robbins
http://www.foodrevolution.org/bio.htm

Daniel Vitalis
http://www.danielvitalis.com/

Dr. Stewart Blaikie
http://www.loveyourliver.org/lyl/

Nadine Artemis
http://www.livinglibations.com/

Truth Calkins
http://www.truthcalkins.com/

Gabriel Cousins
http://www.gabrielcousens.com/

Tree of Life Rejuvenation Center
http://www.treeoflife.nu/home-index/

Hippocrates Health Institute
http://www.hippocratesinst.org/

LifeVantage
http://www.mylifevantage.com/flow

Sustainable Design, Appropriate Technology, Organics and Remediation

Cradle to Cradle by William McDonough and Michael Braumguard
http://www.mcdonough.com/

Solartopia by Harvey Wasserman
http://www.solartopia.org/

Earthships
    http://www.earthship.net/

Paul Stamets
    http://www.fungi.com/

Global Exchange
    http://www.globalexchange.org/

Organic Consumer Association
    http://www.organicconsumers.org/

The Solutions Interactive Documentary Series
    http://www.thesolutionsdoc.com/

Bioneers
    http://www.bioneers.org/

Beyond Nuclear
    http://www.beyondnuclear.org/

Foundations

Common Ground Relief
    http://www.commongroundrelief.org/

The Fruit Tree Planting Foundation
    http://www.ftpf.org/

Medical Education Cooperation with Cuba
    http://www.medicc.org/ns/

Social/Environmental Investment Opportunities

Rocky Mountain Humane Investing
    http://www.greeninvestment.com/home.html

Green For All
    http://www.greenforall.org/

Winslow Green Mutual Funds
    http://www.winslowgreen.com/home/

Green Stocks
    http://www.sustainablebusiness.com/